Emeril Lagasse Power Air Fryer 360 Cookbook

Quick and Tasty Everyday Recipes for Beginners and Advanced Users

Carol Mossi

Table of Contents

Introduction

Air fryers have been all the rage in the last few years.

Consumers love them because they are small, versatile, and can handle even the more challenging recipes. Air fryers are often compared to convection ovens since they cook the same way.

Air fryers usually have a single heating element on top while convection ovens have three.

The Emeril Lagasse Power Air Fryer 360 is powered by a 1500-watt motor and has five heating elements.

It has an impressive 12 cooking presets, a memory function, an extra-large capacity, and an elegant and durable brushed stainless-steel body.

If you're thinking of getting an air fryer, maybe just hold off for a while and find out why an air fryer oven might be the better choice for you.

Chapter 1: Overview of Air Fryer Oven

How Does the Emeril Lagasse Power Air Fryer 360 Work?

Air fryers cook food using the hot air produced by the heating elements. Much like convection ovens, the hot air is circulated by convection fans to cook the food evenly on all sides.

The Emeril Lagasse Power Air Fryer 360 has 5 heating elements located at the top, bottom, and side. Depending on the cooking function selected, the unit will use different heating elements that will yield the best result.

It has a total of 12 presets air fry, toast, pizza, broil, bake, bagel, rotisserie, dehydrate, roast, reheat, warm, and slow cook. There are four levels between the top and bottom heating elements where you can place your tray, rack, or pan when cooking. The guide is conveniently printed on the glass door for reference too.

The first position, nearest the top heating element is ideal for broiling and dehydrating. The second position can be used for toast, bagel, broil, air fry, dehydrate, and rotisserie functions. The third position is for using the reheat, bake, roast, warm, pizza, and dehydrate functions. Finally, the fourth position is for the slow cook function.

Programs and Functions

- Air fry

The air fry function will use the side heating elements with the air fry fans turned on for the entire process. The crisper tray must be placed in the second position. When cooking foods that have sufficient moisture or fat content that may drip during the cooking process, it is best to use the baking tray and pizza rack just below the crisper tray.

- Toast

The toast function uses the top and bottom heating elements to make those toasted brown coloration on both sides. You can select how dark your toast should be from levels one to five. It can toast six loaf bread slices at a time.

- Bagel

The bagel function uses the top and bottom heating elements while the air frying fans are turned off during the process. Like the toast function, you can fit up to six slices of bagels and select the darkness of the toast. The pizza rack is placed in the second position when using this function.

- Pizza

The pizza function uses the top and bottom heating elements. The bottom heating element makes the dough crispy, while the top melts the cheese and cooks the toppings. The air frying fans may be turned on during the cooking process.

- Bake

Ideal for baking pastries, cakes, and pies, the bake function uses the top and bottom heating elements and provides the option of turning the air frying fans on or off.

- Broil

The broil function is perfect for searing and melting cheeses over burgers, sandwiches, or fries. It uses the top heating element while the air frying fan is turned off. The pizza rack must be placed near the top heating element to get the best results.

- Rotisserie

The rotisserie function uses both the top and bottom heating elements together with the rotating spit accessory. Food becomes brown and crispy outside while soft and juicy inside.

- Slow cook

The slow cook function uses the top and bottom heating elements. It is perfect for making tender pulled pork or beef brisket and is best used with a Dutch oven, baking dish with lid, or any similar cooking pot. The Power Air Fryer 360 is capable of up to 10 hours of slow cooking.

- Roast

For cooking large cuts of meat, the roast function is the more suitable preset as it evenly cooks the meat on all sides. It also uses the top and bottom heating elements.

- Dehydrate

The dehydrate function is perfect for drying fruits, vegetables, and meat. It only uses the top heating element with the air frying fans turned on during the entire process to evenly dry out the ingredients.

- Reheat

The reheat function uses both the top and bottom heating elements with the option to turn on the air frying fans. It is ideal for reheating food items without searing it.

- Warm

The warm function uses the top and bottom heating elements with the air frying fans turned off. It is ideal for keeping the food within a safe temperature until you are ready to serve it.

Benefits of Air Fryer Oven Cooking

1. Compact and versatile

Compared to conventional ovens, air fryer ovens can easily fit in your kitchen countertop and can be stored when not in use. They are versatile and can perform several cooking functions.

2. Energy-efficient

Air fryer ovens can heat up and cook 40% faster than bulky, conventional ovens.

3. Rotisserie function

Let's you cook an entire chicken, a lamb leg, a large chunk of beef, or several kebabs with ease. Some air fryer ovens come with a rotisserie spit or drum that makes roasting meat or any other food so much easier.

4. Bigger capacity than standard air fryers

The interior has different levels that let you cook different foods at the same time. The Power Air Fryer 360 alone can cook a whole chicken in under an hour.

5. Requires much less oil than traditional cookers

Air fryers use 70% less oil than standard deep fryers making it a more economical and healthier choice.

Tips for Cooking Success

- Make sure that you follow the initial steps required before using the appliance.
- Foods that are smaller in size will require less cooking time. If you want to cut down on cooking time, cutting food into similar sizes will guarantee faster and even cooking.
- Spraying, misting, or lightly coating, food with oil before cooking will create a crispier texture. Be careful not to put too much, or it will turn soggy instead.
- Make sure that you flip or stir the food halfway through the cooking time to get even cooking.
- Snack or pastry recipes intended for conventional ovens may also be made in the air fryer oven.
- Avoid overcrowding the food. Leave some space in between, especially when cooking food with coating or batter, to let the hot air circulate and cook the food on all sides.
- For recipes that require high temperatures, it is better to use oils that have a high smoking point or that can withstand high temperatures. Avocado, peanut, and grapeseed oils are excellent examples of this. Olive oil has a low smoke point. If you must use olive oil, use extra light olive oil as it has a higher smoke point and will not dry up the food before it cooks.
- Do not place cooking trays or pans directly on the bottom heating elements as this will prevent the hot air to properly circulate and cook food.

- Crumbs and drippings like oil and grease can create smoke and burn. To prevent this, put a baking tray lined with foil and parchment paper and place it below the crisper tray or baking pan.

Guidelines for Safety and Precautions

One of the most first things to do upon getting your unit is to read the user's manual. Not only will it guide you with the proper usage, but it will also save you from any mishap during operation. Below are some of the guidelines to remember when using your Emeril Lagasse Power Air Fryer.

DO

- The appliance is intended to be used indoors only.
- The appliance must only be operated by persons without any reduced sensory, mental, or physical capabilities and has read and understood the manual.
- Place away from wet areas and hot surfaces such as stovetops.
- Place the air fryer oven in a stable, level, and heat-resistant countertop or table.
- Leave at least five inches of space all around the oven, as it may heat up and release steam during operation.
- Make sure that there's no food protruding from the oven while in use.
- Use oven mitts, gloves, or dish towels when taking out food.
- Turn the appliance off properly before carefully unplugging the unit.
- Unplug and clean the appliance after each use.
- Take out and clean the drip tray when is filled halfway.
- Exercise caution when disposing of any hot oil from the unit.
- Wait for the unit to cool down completely for at least 30 minutes after unplugging.

DO NOT

- Use an extension cord with this appliance to prevent accidents.
- Use the unit without the drip tray installed.
- Place anything on top of the oven.
- Block the air vents, especially while the unit is turned on.

- Put flammable materials near or on top of the air fryer oven such as paper, plastic, curtains, towels, etc.
- Connect to an electrical outlet that is already used by other appliances as it may cause it to overload.
- Connect with an electrical outlet other than a 2-prong grounded 120V.
- Modify the plug or any part of the unit.
- Use accessories that are not recommended by the manufacturer.
- Clean parts with metal scouring pads and abrasive chemicals.
- Submerge the unit in water.
- Line the drip tray with foil.
- Use metal utensils or cutleries to prevent electric shock.

Follow the steps below when you are about to use the unit for the first time.

1. Before using your air fryer oven for the first time, all packing materials, labels, and stickers must be removed and disposed of properly.
2. Wash the crisper tray, drip tray, pizza rack, baking pan, rotisserie spit, and rotisserie stand with warm water and a mild detergent. Dry thoroughly.
3. Clean the exterior and interior with a damp cloth with some mild detergent. Make sure that the cloth is not too wet, otherwise, it might soak some electrical parts with water.
4. Plug the unit in an outlet located on top of the kitchen counter.
5. Preheat the oven for a few minutes to burn off any protective coating or oil. It is normal for some smoke to appear during this stage.
6. Turn off the unit, unplug, and let it cool down completely. Wipe the interior and exterior again with a damp cloth.

Chapter 2: Breakfast Recipes

Quiche Lorraine

Preparation Time: 15 minutes
Cooking Time: 32 minutes
Servings: 6

Ingredients:

- 1 tablespoon butter
- ½ cup onion, diced
- 2 oz. button mushrooms
- ¼ cup ham, diced
- ¾ cup cream
- 1 egg yolk
- 1 egg
- ½ teaspoon thyme
- ¼ teaspoon ground nutmeg
- Salt and pepper to taste
- ½ cup Gruyere cheese, grated
- 1 refrigerated pie crust

Method:

1. Add the butter to a pan over medium heat.
2. Cook the onion and mushrooms for 5 minutes, stirring often.
3. Stir in the ham, cream, egg yolk and egg.
4. Season with the thyme, nutmeg, salt and pepper.
5. Cook for 2 minutes.
6. Add the pie crust to a pie pan.
7. Pour the mixture into the pie crust.
8. Sprinkle the cheese on top.
9. Place the pan inside the Emeril Air Fryer.

10. Choose bake setting.
11. Set it to 300 degrees F.
12. Cook for 25 minutes.

Serving Suggestions: Let cool for 20 minutes before slicing and serving.

Preparation & Cooking Tips: You can also use Swiss cheese for this recipe.

Cheesy Biscuits

Preparation Time: 10 minutes

Cooking Time: 10 minutes

Servings: 6

Ingredients:

- ½ cup cake flour
- 1 ¼ cups all-purpose flour
- ½ teaspoon baking soda
- ¾ teaspoon baking powder
- ¼ cup butter, sliced into cubes
- ½ cup cheddar, grated
- 1 teaspoon sugar
- ¾ cup buttermilk
- 3 tablespoons scallions, chopped

Method:

1. Sift the flours, baking soda and baking powder into a bowl.
2. Stir in the rest of the ingredients.
3. Mix.
4. Form round shapes from the dough.
5. Press down to flatten.
6. Place the biscuits in a baking pan.
7. Slide it inside the Emeril Air Fryer.
8. Select air fry setting.
9. Cook at 400 degrees F for 8 to 10 minutes.

Serving Suggestions: Serve with softened butter.

Preparation & Cooking Tips: Extend cooking time if you want your biscuits crispy on the edges.

Breakfast Tuna Melt

Preparation Time: 15 minutes
Cooking Time: 12 minutes
Servings: 4

Ingredients:

- ½ cup onion, chopped
- ½ cup mayonnaise
- 2 oz. canned tuna flakes in water, drained
- ¼ teaspoon dried Italian herbs
- Salt and pepper to taste
- 1 ½ tablespoons lemon juice
- 10 slices ciabatta bread
- 10 oz. Provolone cheese slices
- 10 slices tomato

Method:

1. Mix the onion, mayo, tuna, herbs, salt, pepper and lemon juice in a bowl.
2. Spread mixture on top of the bread slices.
3. Top with the cheese and tomato.
4. Place in the crisper tray.
5. Choose air fry setting.
6. Cook at 400 degrees F for 12 minutes.

Serving Suggestions: Serve with potato chips.

Preparation & Cooking Tips: Use freshly squeezed lemon juice.

Baked Apple Toast

Preparation Time: 5 minutes
Cooking Time: 5 minutes
Servings: 2

Ingredients:

- 1 tablespoon butter, melted
- 2 slices bread
- 1 teaspoon ground cinnamon
- 3 tablespoons apple, diced

Method:

1. Spread the butter on top of the bread.
2. Sprinkle with the cinnamon.
3. Place the chopped apples on top.
4. Add the toasts to the air crisper tray.
5. Press toast setting.
6. Cook at 330 degrees F for 5 minutes.

Serving Suggestions: Drizzle with honey before serving.

Preparation & Cooking Tips: Use whole wheat or rye bread for this recipe.

Ricotta Toast

Preparation Time: 10 minutes
Cooking Time: 8 minutes
Servings: 2

Ingredients:

- ¼ cup walnuts, diced
- 1 clove garlic, minced
- 1 cup cherry tomatoes, sliced in half
- 2 tablespoons olive oil
- Salt and pepper to taste
- 2 slices bread
- ½ cup ricotta cheese
- 2 tablespoons Parmesan cheese, grated

Method:

1. Toss the walnuts, garlic and tomatoes in olive oil.
2. Season with salt and pepper.
3. Add the mixture to the air crisper tray.
4. Cook at 330 degrees F for 5 minutes.
5. Transfer the mixture on top of the bread slices.
6. Top with cheeses.
7. Set the air fryer to toast.
8. Cook for 3 minutes.

Serving Suggestions: Sprinkle with chopped parsley or green onions.

Preparation & Cooking Tips: Replace walnuts with almonds if walnuts are not available.

Cinnamon French Toast

Preparation Time: 5 minutes
Cooking Time: 6 minutes
Servings: 4

Ingredients:

- 2/3 cup of milk
- 2 eggs, beaten
- ½ teaspoon ground cinnamon
- 1 teaspoon vanilla
- 4 slices bread

Method:

1. In a bowl, mix all the ingredients except bread.
2. Dip the bread in the mixture.
3. Place in the air crisper tray.
4. Set it to air fry.
5. Cook at 320 degrees F for 3 minutes per side.

Serving Suggestions: Serve with maple syrup or honey.

Preparation & Cooking Tips: Soak the bread in the mixture for 30 seconds before air frying.

German Pancake

Preparation Time: 5 minutes
Cooking Time: 6 minutes
Servings: 2

Ingredients:

- ¼ cup all-purpose flour
- ½ cup milk
- 2 eggs
- 1 teaspoon baking soda
- 1 teaspoon vanilla extract
- 1 teaspoon sugar

Method:

1. Combine all the ingredients in a bowl.
2. Pour the ingredients in a baking pan.
3. Place it in the air fryer.
4. Choose air fry setting.
5. Cook at 350 degrees F for 3 minutes.
6. Flip and cook for another 3 minutes.

Serving Suggestions: Dust with powdered sugar.

Preparation & Cooking Tips: Let batter sit at room temperature for 15 minutes before air frying.

Breakfast Quesadilla

Preparation Time: 10 minutes
Cooking Time: 5 minutes
Servings: 2

Ingredients:

- 1 cup cooked scrambled eggs
- 2 slices bacon, cooked crisp and crumbled
- ¼ cup cheddar cheese, shredded
- 4 flour tortillas

Method:

1. Add the eggs on top of the 2 tortillas.
2. Top with the cheese and bacon.
3. Place the other tortillas on top.
4. Place in the air crisper tray.
5. Select air fry function.
6. Cook at 310 degrees F for 5 minutes.

Serving Suggestions: Sprinkle with chopped parsley.

Preparation & Cooking Tips: Use turkey bacon to reduce calorie and fat content.

Scrambled Egg Toast

Preparation Time: 5 minutes
Cooking Time: 5 minutes
Servings: 2

Ingredients:

- 2 slices bread
- 2 tablespoons butter
- 1 cup scrambled eggs

Method:

1. Spread the butter on top of the bread.
2. Add the scrambled eggs on top.
3. Place in the air fryer.
4. Set it to air fry.
5. Cook at 330 degrees F for 5 minutes.

Serving Suggestions: Sprinkle chopped chives on top.

Preparation & Cooking Tips: Use sourdough bread if available.

Cheesy Egg Toast

Preparation Time: 5 minutes
Cooking Time: 7 minutes
Servings: 2

Ingredients:

- 2 slices bread
- 2 eggs
- ¼ cup cheddar cheese, shredded
- Salt and pepper to taste

Method:

1. Make a hole in the middle of the bread using a cookie cutter.
2. Place these in the air fryer tray.
3. Crack the eggs into the hole.
4. Sprinkle cheese, salt and pepper on top.
5. Choose air fry function.
6. Cook at 350 degrees F for 5 minutes.

Serving Suggestions: Sprinkle chopped green onions on top.

Preparation & Cooking Tips: You can also use mozzarella cheese on top

Chapter 3: Beef Recipes

Flank Steak

Preparation Time: 6 hours and 20 minutes
Cooking Time: 20 minutes
Servings: 4

Ingredients:

Chimichurri

- 1 cup olive oil
- 3 tablespoons garlic, minced
- ¼ cup fresh basil leaves, chopped
- 2 tablespoons lime juice
- ½ cup vinegar
- 1 tablespoon marjoram leaves, chopped
- 1 cup cilantro, chopped
- 2 tablespoons shallots, minced

Steak

- 2 lb. flank steak
- Salt and pepper to taste

Method:

1. Mix the chimichurri ingredients in a food processor.
2. Pulse until well combined.
3. Season the flank steak with salt and pepper.
4. Spread 1 cup chimichurri on both sides of steaks.
5. Cover and refrigerate for 6 hours.
6. Add the steaks to the pizza rack.
7. Select air fry function.

8. Cook at 400 degrees F for 18 to 20 minutes.
9. Serve with remaining chimichurri.

Serving Suggestions: Serve with crusty bread.

Preparation & Cooking Tips: Use sherry wine vinegar if available.

Korean Beef

Preparation Time: 10 minutes

Cooking Time: 10 minutes

Servings: 4

Ingredients:

- 1 tablespoon   garlic, minced
- 1 tablespoon   ginger, minced
- 2 tablespoons orange juice
- ¼ cup soy sauce
- 1 tablespoon   red pepper flakes
- 1 cup scallions
- 1 tablespoon brown sugar
- 2 teaspoons sesame oil
- 1 lb. sirloin steaks

Method:

1. Combine all the ingredients in a bowl.
2. Cover and marinate the steak for 4 hours.
3. Place the steak in the air crisper tray.
4. Slice it inside the air fryer oven.
5. Choose air fry setting.
6. Cook at 400 degrees F for 10 minutes.

Serving Suggestions: Serve with steamed white rice and kimchi.

Preparation & Cooking Tips: You can also wrap the beef in lettuce leaves.

Giant Burger

Preparation Time: 20 minutes
Cooking Time: 40 minutes
Servings: 4

Ingredients:

Patty

- 3 lb. ground beef
- 8 oz. bacon, cooked crispy and chopped
- 1 tablespoon   Creole seasoning
- Salt and pepper to taste

Burger

- 2 pizza crusts
- 1 cup Monterey Jack cheese, shredded
- 1 cup cheddar cheese, shredded
- ¼ cup onion, diced
- ¼ cup dill pickles, diced

Method:

1. Mix the patty ingredients in a bowl.
2. Form a big patty from the mixture.
3. Add the patty to the crisper tray.
4. Place it inside the air fryer oven.
5. Press bake setting.
6. Cook for 25 minutes.
7. Transfer the patty on top of the pizza crust
8. Top with the cheese onion and pickles.
9. Top with the other pizza crust.
10. Add the giant burger inside the air fryer oven.

11. Press toast.

12. Toast for 15 minutes.

Serving Suggestions: Brush top with butter and sprinkle with sesame seeds before serving.

Preparation & Cooking Tips: You can also use a combination of ground beef and ground pork for the patty.

Roast Beef

Preparation Time: 15 minutes
Cooking Time: 1 hour and 15 minutes
Servings: 6

Ingredients:

- 1 lb. beef roast
- Salt and pepper to taste
- 1 tablespoon Creole seasoning
- 3 tablespoons olive oil
- 1 onion, sliced
- 5 cloves garlic, crushed
- 3 sprigs thyme
- 2 cup beef broth
- 3 tablespoons butter, softened
- 3 tablespoons flour

Method:

1. Sprinkle all sides of the roast with salt, pepper and Creole seasoning.
2. Add the olive oil to a pan over medium heat.
3. Brown the roast on all sides.
4. Add the onion, garlic and thyme.
5. Pour in the broth.
6. Simmer for 10 minutes.
7. Transfer the beef to a baking pan.
8. Slide into the air fryer oven.
9. Choose roast setting.
10. Cook at 325 degrees F for 1 hour.
11. Add the butter and flour to the cooking liquid in the pan.
12. Simmer for 5 minutes.
13. Pour the sauce over the roast and serve.

Serving Suggestions: Let rest for 15 minutes before slicing and serving.

Steak Roulade

Preparation Time: 10 minutes
Cooking Time: 35 minutes
Servings: 4

Ingredients:

- 1 tablespoon olive oil
- 4 cups spinach
- 3 cloves garlic, sliced
- 2 lb. flank steak, butterflied
- Salt and pepper to taste
- 9 slices cheddar cheese
- 1 ½ cups roasted peppers

Method:

1. Pour olive oil into a pan over medium heat.
2. Cook the garlic and spinach for 2 minutes.
3. Season steak with salt and pepper.
4. Top each steak with spinach, cheese and peppers.
5. Roll the steak and secure with a kitchen string.
6. Attach the roulade to the rotisserie spit.
7. Set the air fryer oven to rotisserie function.
8. Set it to 375 degrees F for 30 minutes.

Serving Suggestions: Let roulade rest for 10 minutes before serving.

Preparation & Cooking Tips: You can also use other types of cheese for this recipe.

Blue Cheese Burger

Preparation Time: 20 minutes
Cooking Time: 30 minutes
Servings: 4

Ingredients:

- 2 lb. ground beef
- Salt and pepper to taste
- 2 tablespoon   Worcestershire sauce
- 4 slices bacon, cooked crisp and crumbled
- 8 tablespoons blue cheese, crumbled
- ¼ cup butter
- 4 burger buns, toasted
- 4 lettuce leaves
- 4 slices red onions
- 8 slices tomatoes

Method:

1. Mix the beef, salt, pepper and Worcestershire sauce.
2. Form patties from the mixture.
3. Stuff the patties with the blue cheese and bacon.
4. Place the patties on the pizza rack.
5. Choose air fry setting.
6. Cook at 400 degrees F for 18 to 20 minutes.
7. Spread butter on the burger buns.
8. Top with the patties, lettuce, onion and tomatoes.
9. Toast in the oven for 10 minutes.

Serving Suggestions: Serve with mustard.

Preparation & Cooking Tips: Use Romaine lettuce if available.

Grilled Steak

Preparation Time: 10 minutes
Cooking Time: 12 minutes
Servings: 1

Ingredients:

- 1 rib eye steak
- 1 teaspoon steak seasoning
- Pepper to taste

Method:

1. Season steak with steak seasoning and pepper.
2. Set the air fryer oven to grill.
3. Add the steak to the pan.
4. Cook for 5 to 6 minutes per side.

Serving Suggestions: Let steak rest for 5 minutes before slicing and serving.

Preparation & Cooking Tips: Let the steak rest at room temperature for 10 minutes before seasoning.

Rib Eye Steak with Garlic Butter

Preparation Time: 10 minutes

Cooking Time: 10 minutes

Servings: 2

Ingredients:

- 2 rib eye steaks
- 2 tablespoons butter, melted
- Garlic powder to taste
- Pepper to taste

Method:

1. Brush the rib eye steaks with butter.
2. Season with garlic powder and pepper.
3. Set your air fryer oven to air fry.
4. Preheat it to 400 degrees F.
5. Cook for 5 minutes per side.

Serving Suggestions: Drizzle additional butter over the steaks before serving.

Preparation & Cooking Tips: You can also flavor the steak with minced garlic and butter.

Sirloin with Rosemary, Basil & Garlic

Preparation Time: 10 minutes

Cooking Time: 12 minutes

Servings: 2

Ingredients:

- 2 sirloin steaks
- 2 tablespoons butter, melted
- Salt and pepper to taste
- 3 sprigs rosemary
- ½ cup butter, melted
- ½ teaspoon garlic powder
- 1 teaspoon fresh parsley, chopped
- 4 teaspoons fresh basil, chopped

Method:

1. Set your air fryer oven to air fry.
2. Brush the steaks with the butter.
3. Season with the salt and pepper.
4. Place inside the air fryer oven.
5. Top with the rosemary sprigs.
6. Cook at 400 degrees F for 6 minutes per side.
7. In a bowl, mix the remaining butter, garlic powder, parsley and basil.
8. Pour the herbed butter over the steaks and serve.

Serving Suggestions: Serve with mashed potatoes and gravy.

Preparation & Cooking Tips: Let steaks rest for 10 minutes before seasoning.

Beef Teriyaki

Preparation Time: 10 minutes
Cooking Time: 15 minutes
Servings: 4

Ingredients:

- ¼ cup vegetable oil
- 1 cup soy sauce
- 1 ½ cups brown sugar
- ½ cup pineapple juice
- 1 teaspoon garlic powder
- ½ cup water
- 2 lb. top round steak, sliced into strips

Method:

1. Combine all the ingredients except steak in a bowl.
2. Soak the steak strips in the mixture.
3. Cover and refrigerate overnight.
4. Place it inside the air fryer oven.
5. Choose air fry setting.
6. Cook at 400 degrees for 5 to 7 minutes per side.

Serving Suggestions: Garnish with white sesame seeds.

Preparation & Cooking Tips: You can also use sirloin strips for this recipe.

Chapter 4: Pork Recipes

Vietnamese Pork Rolls

Preparation Time: 20 minutes
Cooking Time: 20 minutes
Servings: 4

Ingredients:

- 2 tablespoons vegetable oil
- ½ cup yellow onion, chopped
- 1 tablespoon   garlic, minced
- ¼ lb. ground pork
- 1 tablespoon scallions, chopped
- 1 cup carrot, sliced into thin strips
- 1 cup bean sprouts
- 1 cup mint
- 1 cup cilantro
- 24 spring roll wrappers
- ¼ cup lime juice
- 2 tablespoon   fish sauce
- 1 tablespoon chili garlic sauce

Method:

1. Add oil to a pan over medium heat.
2. Cook onion, garlic and ground pork for 8 to 10 minutes, stirring frequently.
3. Stir in the scallions, carrot, bean sprouts, mint and cilantro.
4. Cook for 3 minutes, stirring often.
5. Drain the mixture.
6. Top the wrappers with the mixture.
7. Roll up the wrappers and seal.
8. Add the rolls to the crisper tray.

9. Choose air fry setting.
10. Cook at 380 degrees F for 7 minutes.
11. Mix lime juice and fish sauce.
12. Serve rolls with lime juice mixture and chili garlic.

Serving Suggestions: Garnish with chopped green onions.

Preparation & Cooking Tips: Use freshly squeezed lime juice.

Bacon Pudding with Corn

Preparation Time: 20 minutes
Cooking Time: 25 minutes
Servings: 6

Ingredients:

- 4 slices bacon
- 1 onion, chopped
- 2 teaspoons garlic, minced
- 1 red bell pepper, diced
- ¼ cup celery, chopped
- 1 cup corn kernels
- ¾ teaspoon Creole seasoning
- Pinch cayenne pepper
- Salt to taste
- 3 eggs, beaten
- ½ cup heavy cream
- 1 ½ cups milk
- 1 tablespoon   butter
- 3 cups day old bread, sliced into cubes
- 1 cup Monterey Jack cheese, grated

Method:

1. Cook the bacon in a pan over medium heat.
2. Stir in the onion, garlic, red bell pepper, celery, corn, Creole seasoning, cayenne pepper and salt.
3. Cook for 5 minutes, stirring often.
4. In a bowl, mix the eggs, cream and milk.
5. Fold in butter, bread, cheese and onion mixture.
6. Pour the pudding into a casserole dish.
7. Slide it into the pizza rack.

8. Choose bake setting.
9. Cook at 325 degrees F for 20 minutes.

Serving Suggestions: Sprinkle with Parmesan cheese before serving.

Preparation & Cooking Tips: You can also add thyme to the mixture.

Spicy Short Ribs

Preparation Time: 20 minutes
Cooking Time: 8 hours
Servings: 5

Ingredients:

- 6 lb. beef short ribs
- Salt and pepper to taste
- 14 oz. ketchup
- 12 oz. beer
- 1 tablespoon molasses
- 1 tablespoon mustard
- 2 cloves garlic, minced
- ½ cup onions, chopped
- ¼ cup brown sugar
- 1 teaspoon hot pepper sauce
- 1 teaspoon cayenne pepper

Method:

1. Season ribs with salt and pepper.
2. Add the ribs to a Dutch oven.
3. Add the rest of the ingredients to a food processor.
4. Pulse until smooth.
5. Coat the ribs with the mixture.
6. Place the ribs and sauce in the pizza rack.
7. Choose slow cook setting.
8. Cook at 225 degrees F for 8 hours.

Serving Suggestions: Garnish with chopped green onions.

Preparation & Cooking Tips: Use whole grain mustard if available.

Pork Roast

Preparation Time: 10 minutes

Cooking Time: 1 hour

Servings: 6

Ingredients:

- 2 tablespoons orange juice
- 1 tablespoon orange zest
- ½ cup brown sugar
- ½ cup honey
- Salt and pepper to taste
- 4 lb. pork loin roast

Method:

1. Add all the ingredients except pork in a bowl.
2. Mix well.
3. Attach the rotisserie spit through the pork.
4. Place it in the air fryer oven.
5. Coat the pork with the mixture.
6. Choose rotisserie setting.
7. Cook at 350 degrees F for 1 hour, basting the pork every 15 minutes.

Serving Suggestions: Let pork rest for 15 minutes before slicing and serving.

Preparation & Cooking Tips: You can add ¼ cup to the mixture.

Pork Teriyaki

Preparation Time: 10 minutes
Cooking Time: 20 minutes
Servings: 4

Ingredients:

- 1 tablespoon vegetable oil
- 2 tablespoons soy sauce
- 1 tablespoon brown sugar
- 1 tablespoon dry sherry
- 1 clove garlic, minced
- 1 tablespoon vinegar
- 1 teaspoon ginger, grated
- Salt and pepper to taste
- 1 lb. pork tenderloin

Method:

1. Add all the ingredients except pork in a bowl.
2. Mix well.
3. Add pork to the bowl.
4. Cover and marinate overnight.
5. Cook at 400 degrees F for 20 to 30 minutes, flipping once.

Serving Suggestions: Let rest for 15 minutes before slicing.

Preparation & Cooking Tips: Use rice vinegar if available.

Savory Pork Loin

Preparation Time: 5 minutes
Cooking Time: 5 minutes
Servings: 4

Ingredients:

- 4 slices pork loin
- Garlic salt to taste
- Pepper to taste

Method:

1. Season pork loin with garlic salt and pepper.
2. Place pork loin in the air crisper tray.
3. Choose air fry setting.
4. Set it to 320 degrees F.
5. Cook for 5 to 8 minutes.

Serving Suggestions: Serve with vinegar and chili sauce.

Preparation & Cooking Tips: Internal temperature of pork should reach 145 degrees F.

Breaded Pork Chops

Preparation Time: 5 minutes
Cooking Time: 12 minutes
Servings: 4

Ingredients:

- 4 pork chops
- Salt and pepper to taste
- 1 egg, beaten
- Cooking spray

Breading

- 1 cup bread crumbs
- 2/3 cups cornflakes, crushed
- 2 teaspoons sweet paprika
- 1 teaspoon garlic powder
- 1 teaspoon onion powder
- 1 teaspoon chili powder

Method:

1. Season the pork chops with salt and pepper.
2. Dip in egg.
3. In a bowl, mix the breading ingredients.
4. Cover the pork chops with the breading.
5. Spray with oil.
6. Add the pork chops to the air crisper tray.
7. Cook at 360 degrees F for 6 minutes per side.

Serving Suggestions: Serve with hot sauce and mustard.

Preparation & Cooking Tips: You can use either bone-in or boneless pork chops.

Ham with Apricot Sauce

Preparation Time: 5 minutes
Cooking Time: 10 minutes
Servings: 2

Ingredients:

- 1 teaspoon lemon juice
- 1 teaspoon lemon juice
- ¼ cup apricot preserves
- ½ teaspoon ground cinnamon
- 1 teaspoon mustard
- 2 ham steaks

Method:

1. Mix the ingredients in a bowl except the ham.
2. Brush ham with the sauce.
3. Place the ham steaks in the air crisper tray.
4. Select air fry setting.
5. Cook at 350 degrees F for 5 minutes per side, basting with the sauce.

Serving Suggestions: Garnish with chopped green onions.

Preparation & Cooking Tips: Use Dijon style mustard.

Pork & Veggies

Preparation Time: 20 minutes
Cooking Time: 20 minutes
Servings: 4

Ingredients:

Veggies

- ½ cup onion, diced
- 10 oz. mushrooms, diced
- 2 red peppers, diced
- 1 lb. cabbage, shredded
- 1 tablespoon olive oil
- 1 tablespoon Cajun seasoning

Pork

- 1 lb. pork tenderloin
- Salt and pepper to taste

Method:

1. Toss the veggies in oil and seasoning.
2. Add to the air crisper tray.
3. Select air fry setting.
4. Cook at 350 degrees F for 5 minutes.
5. Stir and cook for another 5 minutes.
6. Transfer to a serving plate.
7. Season pork with salt and pepper.
8. Set it inside the air fryer oven.
9. Cook at 350 degrees F for 10 minutes, flipping once.
10. Serve pork with veggies.

Serving Suggestions: Sprinkle with pepper before serving.

Blackened Pork Chops

Preparation Time: 5 minutes
Cooking Time: 15 minutes
Servings: 4

Ingredients:

- 1 lb. pork loins

Dry rub

- 1 teaspoon chili powder
- 1 teaspoon paprika
- 1 teaspoon cayenne pepper
- 1 teaspoon garlic powder
- 1 teaspoon dried thyme
- 1 teaspoon sugar
- Salt to taste

Method:

1. Mix rub ingredients in a bowl.
2. Season both sides of pork with this mixture.
3. Add the pork loin to the air crisper tray.
4. Cook at 360 degrees F for 7 minutes per side.

Serving Suggestions: Serve with your choice of dip.

Preparation & Cooking Tips: Internal temperature should be 145 degrees F.

Chapter 5: Lamb Recipes

Roasted Leg of Lamb

Preparation Time: 20 minutes
Cooking Time: 1 hour and 10 minutes
Servings: 8

Ingredients:

- 1 lb. leg of lamb
- ¼ cup garlic, minced
- 3 tablespoons oregano, chopped
- 2 tablespoons fresh rosemary, chopped
- 1 tablespoon Creole seasoning
- Salt and pepper to taste

Method:

1. Season the lamb with garlic, oregano, rosemary, Creole seasoning, salt and pepper.
2. Tie it with butcher's twine.
3. Attach it to the rotisserie spit.
4. Choose rotisserie setting.
5. Cook at 375 degrees F for 70 minutes.

Serving Suggestions: Serve with sautéed vegetables.

Preparation & Cooking Tips: You can also use dried oregano and dried rosemary for this recipe.

Lamb with Garlic & Rosemary

Preparation Time: 10 minutes
Cooking Time: 25 minutes
Servings: 6

Ingredients:

- 2 tablespoons olive oil
- ¼ cup beef broth
- 5 cloves garlic, minced
- 2 tablespoons fresh rosemary, minced
- Salt and pepper to taste
- 3 lb. leg of lamb

Method:

1. Combine the olive oil, broth, garlic, rosemary, salt and pepper in a bowl.
2. Brush all sides of lamb with the seasoning.
3. Place it in the air crisper.
4. Select air fry setting.
5. Cook at 350 degrees F for 25 minutes.

Serving Suggestions: Serve with your favorite vegetable side dish.

Preparation & Cooking Tips: If you want your lamb well done, internal temperature should be 160 degrees F.

Grilled Lamb Chops

Preparation Time: 5 minutes
Cooking Time: 7 minutes
Servings: 4

Ingredients:

- 4 lamb chops
- 3 tablespoons olive oil
- 4 tablespoons basil, chopped
- 2 teaspoons garlic powder
- Salt and pepper to taste

Method:

1. Brush both sides of the lamb chops with the mixture of olive oil, basil, garlic powder, salt and pepper.
2. Set the lamb chops in the air crisper tray.
3. Turn the knob to grill setting.
4. Cook the lamb chops at 400 degrees F for 7 minutes.
5. Turn and cook for another 7 minutes.

Serving Suggestions: Serve with tomato salad.

Preparation & Cooking Tips: For well-done lamb chops, internal temperature should be at least 150 degrees F.

Greek Lamb Chops

Preparation Time: 15 minutes
Cooking Time: 25 minutes
Servings: 6

Ingredients:

- 2 cloves garlic, minced
- ¼ cup olive oil
- ¼ cup lemon juice
- 2 teaspoon dried oregano
- Salt and pepper to taste
- 2 lb. lamb chops

Method:

1. In a bowl, combine garlic, olive oil, lemon juice, oregano, salt and pepper.
2. Coat both sides of lamb chops with this mixture.
3. Add these to your air fryer oven.
4. Set the air fryer oven to bake.
5. Cook at 350 degrees F for 15 minutes.
6. Flip and cook for another 10 minutes or until fully cooked inside.

Serving Suggestions: Serve with steamed asparagus.

Preparation & Cooking Tips: Use freshly squeezed lemon juice.

Herbed Lamb

Preparation Time: 5 minutes

Cooking Time: 15 minutes

Servings: 4

Ingredients:

- 4 tablespoons olive oil
- 1 teaspoon garlic powder
- 2 tablespoons dried rosemary
- 1 tablespoon dried thyme
- 2 tablespoons parsley, chopped
- Salt and pepper to taste
- 1 rack of lamb

Method:

1. Mix the oil, garlic powder, herbs, salt and pepper in a bowl.
2. Rub the lamb with the mixture.
3. Place it in the air fryer oven.
4. Select air fry setting.
5. Cook at 360 degrees F for 10 minutes.
6. Flip and cook for another 10 minutes.

Serving Suggestions: Serve with grilled corn.

Preparation & Cooking Tips: Internal temperature of rack of lamb should be at least 160 degrees F.

Chapter 6: Chicken Recipes

Spicy Fried Chicken

Preparation Time: 1 day and 30 minutes
Cooking Time: 40 minutes
Servings: 6

Ingredients:

- 3 tablespoons garlic, minced
- ¼ cup hot sauce
- 1 quart buttermilk
- 2 teaspoons celery salt
- Salt and pepper to taste
- 1 lb. chicken, sliced into 6 to 8 pieces
- 4 eggs
- ½ cup milk
- 4 cups flour
- ¾ cup cider vinegar
- 1 tablespoon red pepper flakes
- ½ cup red bell pepper, minced

Method:

1. Mix the garlic, hot sauce, buttermilk, celery salt, salt and pepper in a bowl.
2. Coat the chicken with the mixture.
3. Cover and refrigerate for 1 day.
4. Beat the eggs in a bowl.
5. Stir in the milk.
6. In another bowl, mix the flour, salt and pepper.
7. Dip chicken in the eggs.
8. Cover with flour.
9. Place in the air crisper tray.

10. Select air fry function.

11. Cook at 400 degrees F for 35 to 40 minutes or until golden and crispy.

12. Add vinegar, red pepper flakes and red bell peppers to a food processor.

13. Pulse until smooth.

14. Transfer sauce to a pan.

15. Heat through for 1 minute.

16. Serve chicken with the pepper sauce.

Serving Suggestions: Serve with pasta or rice.

Preparation & Cooking Tips: You can also use fresh chopped red pepper in place of red pepper flakes.

Roasted Chicken

Preparation Time: 20 minutes

Cooking Time: 1 hour

Servings: 4

Ingredients:

- 4 lb. whole chicken

Dry rub

- ½ cup paprika
- ¼ cup garlic powder
- 1/8 cup salt
- ¼ cup pepper
- 3 tablespoons onion powder
- 3 tablespoons ground cayenne pepper
- 3 tablespoons dried thyme
- 3 tablespoons dried oregano

Method:

1. Combine dry rub ingredients in a bowl.
2. Rub chicken using ¼ cup of the dry rub mixture.
3. Truss the whole chicken.
4. Attach it to the rotisserie spit.
5. Place inside the air fryer oven.
6. Choose rotisserie setting.
7. Cook at 350 degrees F for 1 hour.

Serving Suggestions: Let rest for 15 minutes before serving.

Preparation & Cooking Tips: Dry the chicken thoroughly with paper towel before seasoning with herbs and spices.

Chicken with Veggies

Preparation Time: 10 minutes
Cooking Time: 15 minutes
Servings: 2

Ingredients:

Chicken

- 2 chicken breast fillets
- 2 tablespoons olive oil
- 1 tablespoon onion powder
- 1 tablespoon garlic powder
- Salt and pepper to taste

Veggies

- 1 cup cherry tomatoes
- 2 teaspoons olive oil
- 1 cup arugula

Method:

1. Brush the chicken breast fillets with oil.
2. Sprinkle with onion powder, garlic powder, salt and pepper.
3. Place in the air crisper tray.
4. Select air fry function.
5. Cook at 370 degrees F for 4 to 5 minutes per side.
6. Transfer to a plate.
7. Toss the tomatoes in the olive oil.
8. Add to the air fryer tray.
9. Air fry at 350 degrees F for 5 minutes.
10. Serve the chicken with the arugula on the side topped with the roasted tomatoes.

Serving Suggestions: Sprinkle the tomatoes and arugula with Parmesan cheese before serving.

Preparation & Cooking Tips: If not available, use lettuce instead of arugula.

Szechuan Chicken

Preparation Time: 20 minutes
Cooking Time: 10 minutes
Servings: 2

Ingredients:

Chicken

- 1 lb. chicken breast fillet, diced
- ¼ cup cornstarch
- Cooking spray

Sauce

- ¼ teaspoon garlic powder
- 1 tablespoon brown sugar
- 1 tablespoon black bean sauce
- ¼ cup mayonnaise
- 1 teaspoon hoisin
- 2 teaspoon honey
- 1 teaspoon rice wine vinegar
- 1 teaspoon ground Sichuan Peppercorns

Method:

1. Combine the sauce ingredients in a bowl. Set aside.
2. Coat the diced chicken with cornstarch.
3. Spray with oil.
4. Place in the air crisper tray.
5. Set it to air fry.
6. Cook at 350 degrees F for 8 to 10 minutes, turning once.
7. Toss diced chicken in sauce and serve.

Serving Suggestions: Garnish with white sesame seeds.

Preparation & Cooking Tips: Regular peppercorns can be used in place of Sichuan peppercorns if these are not available.

Korean Fried Chicken

Preparation Time: 10 minutes
Cooking Time: 10 minutes
Servings: 4

Ingredients:

Chicken

- ¼ cup water
- ¼ cup flour
- Salt and pepper to taste
- 1 lb. chicken thigh fillet, diced
- Cooking spray

Sauce

- 3 teaspoons gochujang
- 1 tablespoon sugar
- 1 tablespoon vinegar

Method:

1. Mix the water, flour, salt and pepper.
2. Dip chicken in the batter.
3. Spray with oil.
4. Choose air fry setting.
5. Cook at 350 degrees F for 5 to 7 minutes per side.
6. Mix the sauce ingredients.
7. Coat chicken with sauce before serving.

Serving Suggestions: Serve with white rice.

Preparation & Cooking Tips: Use apple cider vinegar if available.

Cajun Chicken

Preparation Time: 10 minutes
Cooking Time: 20 minutes
Servings: 6

Ingredients:

- 6 chicken drumsticks
- Cooking spray

Cajun dry rub

- 1 teaspoon onion powder
- ½ teaspoon garlic powder
- 1 teaspoon paprika
- ½ teaspoon cayenne pepper
- ½ teaspoon dried thyme
- ½ teaspoon dried oregano
- ½ teaspoon dried basil
- Salt and pepper to taste

Method:

1. Combine dry rub ingredients.
2. Spray chicken with oil.
3. Sprinkle all sides with Cajun seasoning.
4. Place these in the air crisper tray.
5. Cook at 400 degrees F for 10 minutes per side.

Serving Suggestions: Serve with hot pepper sauce.

Preparation & Cooking Tips: Internal temperature of chicken should reach 165 degrees F.

Paprika Chicken

Preparation Time: 10 minutes

Cooking Time: 30 minutes

Servings: 6

Ingredients:

- 2 lb. chicken wings
- 2 tablespoons olive oil
- 1 tablespoon paprika
- 1 teaspoon garlic powder
- Salt and pepper to taste

Method:

1. Toss the chicken in olive oil.
2. Season with the paprika, garlic powder, salt and pepper.
3. Place in the air crisper tray.
4. Set the air fryer oven to air fry function.
5. Set the temperature to 400 degrees F.
6. Cook for 15 minutes per side.

Serving Suggestions: Garnish with lemon slices.

Preparation & Cooking Tips: Use smoked paprika.

Stuffed Chicken

Preparation Time: 10 minutes

Cooking Time: 20 minutes

Servings: 2

Ingredients:

- 4 oz. garlic and herb cream cheese
- 2 chicken breast fillets
- 1 tablespoon olive oil
- Pinch dried Italian herbs
- Salt and pepper to taste

Method:

1. Make a slit in the center of the chicken breast to create a pocket.
2. Stuff the pocket with cream cheese.
3. Brush both sides with olive oil.
4. Season with Italian herbs, salt and pepper.
5. Set the stuffed chicken in the air crisper tray.
6. Cook at 370 degrees F for 10 minutes.
7. Flip and cook for another 10 minutes.

Serving Suggestions: Let rest for 5 minutes before serving.

Preparation & Cooking Tips: Check internal temperature of chicken. It should be 165 degrees F.

Lime Chicken

Preparation Time: 10 minutes
Cooking Time: 30 minutes
Servings: 6

Ingredients:

- 1 tablespoon water
- 2 tablespoons lime juice
- 1 teaspoon lime zest
- 2 tablespoons chipotle in adobo sauce
- Salt and pepper to taste
- 2 lb. chicken wings

Method:

1. Combine the water, lime juice, lime zest, chipotle in adobo sauce, salt and pepper.
2. Soak chicken wings in the sauce.
3. Coat evenly.
4. Place the chicken wings in the air crisper tray.
5. Cook at 380 degrees F for 12 minutes per side.
6. Increase temperature to 400 degrees F and cook for another 6 minutes.

Serving Suggestions: Garnish with lime wedges.

Preparation & Cooking Tips: Use freshly squeezed lime juice.

Sesame Chicken

Preparation Time: 15 minutes
Cooking Time: 20 minutes
Servings: 4

Ingredients:

- 1 lb. chicken thigh fillets, diced
- ½ cup potato starch

Sauce

- 2 tablespoons brown sugar
- ¼ cup soy sauce
- 2 tablespoons orange juice
- ¼ cup hoisin sauce
- 1 teaspoon ground ginger
- 1 teaspoon garlic powder
- 1 tablespoon cornstarch mixed with 1 tablespoon water

Method:

1. Cover chicken with potato starch.
2. Place chicken in the air crisper tray.
3. Cook at 350 degrees F for 7 minutes per side.
4. Add the sauce ingredients except cornstarch mixture to a pan over medium heat.
5. Simmer for 3 minutes.
6. Stir in the cornstarch mixture.
7. Simmer for another 3 minutes.

Serving Suggestions: Garnish with chopped green onions.

Preparation & Cooking Tips: Use freshly squeezed orange juice.

Chapter 7: Fish & Seafood Recipes

Crispy Cod Fillet

Preparation Time: 10 minutes
Cooking Time: 30 minutes
Servings: 4

Ingredients:

- 4 cod fillets
- ¼ cup olive oil
- 1 cup pecans
- ½ tablespoon Creole seasoning
- ¼ cup breadcrumbs

Method:

1. Brush both sides of cod fillets with oil.
2. Add the pecans, seasoning and breadcrumbs to your food processor.
3. Pulse until fully combined.
4. Press the breading on both sides of the fish.
5. Place these on the air crisper tray.
6. Choose air fry setting.
7. Cook at 400 degrees F for 18 minutes.
8. Flip and cook for another 12 minutes.

Serving Suggestions: Garnish with chopped scallions.

Preparation & Cooking Tips: If possible, use roasted pecans.

Stuffed Shrimp

Preparation Time: 15 minutes

Cooking Time: 18 minutes

Servings: 6

Ingredients:

- ½ cup yellow onion, minced
- 1 clove garlic, minced
- ¼ cup green bell pepper, minced
- 1 tablespoon   butter
- 3 tablespoons freshly squeezed lemon juice
- 1 tablespoon   Worcestershire sauce
- 1 ½ teaspoon hot sauce
- ¼ cup mayonnaise
- 1 egg, beaten
- ¼ cup celery, minced
- ¼ cup fresh parsley, chopped
- 1 ½ cups butter crackers
- 2 ½ teaspoons Creole seasoning
- Salt and pepper to taste
- 20 large shrimp, peeled, deveined and butterflied
- 3 tablespoons butter, melted

Method:

1. In a pan over medium heat, sauté onion, garlic and bell peppers in butter for 3 minutes.
2. Transfer to a plate and let cool.
3. Stir in the rest of the ingredients except shrimp and butter.
4. Stuff filling into the shrimp.
5. Drizzle with the melted butter.
6. Place in the air crisper tray.

7. Select air fry function.
8. Cook at 400 degrees F for 18 minutes.

Serving Suggestions: Garnish with lemon wedges.

Preparation & Cooking Tips: Try to find jumbo shrimp for this recipe.

Roasted Salmon

Preparation Time: 5 minutes
Cooking Time: 20 minutes
Servings: 4

Ingredients:

- 4 salmon fillets
- 1 tablespoon lemon juice
- 2 tablespoons garlic salt

Method:

1. Drizzle both sides of salmon with lemon juice.
2. Sprinkle with garlic salt.
3. Place the fish on the pizza rack on shelf position 1.
4. Choose roast function.
5. Cook at 350 degrees F for 20 minutes.

Serving Suggestions: Garnish with lemon slices.

Preparation & Cooking Tips: Flip once or twice during cooking.

Indian Butter Shrimp

Preparation Time: 15 minutes

Cooking Time: 5 minutes

Servings: 4

Ingredients:

- 2 tablespoons tomato chutney
- 2 tablespoons tomato paste
- ¼ cup Poblano peppers, sliced
- ¼ cup scallions, chopped
- 1 lb. shrimp, peeled and deveined
- 2 tablespoons butter, melted

Method:

1. Combine all the ingredients except shrimp and butter in a bowl.
2. Coat the shrimp evenly with the mixture.
3. Add the shrimp to air crisper tray.
4. Air fry at 400 degrees F for 5 minutes.
5. Drizzle butter over shrimp.

Serving Suggestions: Sprinkle with chopped green onions on top before serving.

Preparation & Cooking Tips: You can also use regular chili peppers if Poblano peppers are not available.

Honey Garlic Shrimp

Preparation Time: 3 hours and 10 minutes
Cooking Time: 5 minutes
Servings: 4

Ingredients:

- 2 tablespoons olive oil
- 3 tablespoons soy sauce
- 2 cloves garlic, minced
- ½ cup honey
- 1 lb. shrimp, peeled and deveined

Method:

1. Mix the olive oil, soy sauce, garlic and honey in a bowl.
2. Stir in the shrimp.
3. Cover and marinate for 3 hours in the refrigerator.
4. Thread shrimp onto skewers.
5. Place inside the air fryer oven.
6. Cook at 400 degrees F for 5 minutes.

Serving Suggestions: Garnish with chopped parsley.

Preparation & Cooking Tips: It would be a good idea if you can find large shrimp for this recipe.

Honey Lemon Salmon

Preparation Time: 10 minutes
Cooking Time: 10 minutes
Servings: 2

Ingredients:

- 4 tablespoons honey
- Salt and pepper to taste
- 3 tablespoons lemon juice
- ½ cup butter, melted
- 2 salmon fillets

Method:

1. Combine honey, salt, pepper, lemon juice and butter in a bowl.
2. Brush both sides of salmon with the mixture.
3. Transfer fish to the air crisper tray.
4. Select air fry setting.
5. Set the temperature to 390 degrees F.
6. Cook for 7 to 10 minutes, flipping once.

Serving Suggestions: Garnish with lemon wedges.

Preparation & Cooking Tips: You can also marinate first for 1 hour before air frying.

Herbed Tilapia

Preparation Time: 10 minutes
Cooking Time: 10 minutes
Servings: 4

Ingredients:

- 1 teaspoon dried oregano
- 1 teaspoon garlic powder
- 1 teaspoon lemon juice
- Salt to taste
- 4 tilapia fillets
- Cooking spray

Method:

1. Prepare the rub by mixing the oregano, garlic powder, lemon juice and salt.
2. Spray the tilapia with oil.
3. Sprinkle both sides of the fish with the rub.
4. Place these in the air fryer oven.
5. Select air fry function.
6. Cook at 400 degrees F for 4 to 5 minutes per side.

Serving Suggestions: Garnish with chopped scallions.

Preparation & Cooking Tips: You can also use cod or haddock for this recipe.

Cajun Tilapia

Preparation Time: 10 minutes
Cooking Time: 10 minutes
Servings: 2

Ingredients:

- ¼ cup sour cream
- 1 teaspoon water
- 1 tablespoon Old Bay seasoning
- 1 tablespoon cornstarch
- ½ cup breadcrumbs
- 2 tilapia fillets
- Cooking spray

Method:

1. In a bowl, mix sour cream, water and Old Bay seasoning.
2. In another bowl, combine cornstarch and breadcrumbs.
3. Cover the fish with the sour cream mixture.
4. Dredge with the breadcrumb mixture.
5. Spray with oil.
6. Place in the air crisper tray.
7. Choose air fry setting.
8. Cook at 400 degrees F for 5 minutes per side.

Serving Suggestions: Serve with hot sauce and additional sour cream.

Preparation & Cooking Tips: You can also use other white fish fillets for this recipe.

Lemon Crab Cakes

Preparation Time: 35 minutes
Cooking Time: 10 minutes
Servings: 4

Ingredients:

- 8 oz. crab meat
- 1 stalk green onion, chopped
- 2 tablespoons mayonnaise
- 2 tablespoons bread crumbs
- 1 teaspoon lemon zest
- 1 tablespoon lemon juice

Method:

1. Combine all the ingredients in a bowl.
2. Form 4 patties from the mixture.
3. Cover and refrigerate for 30 minutes.
4. Place the patties on the air crisper tray.
5. Turn the knob to air fry setting.
6. Cook at 370 degrees F for 10 minutes, flipping once.

Serving Suggestions: Serve with remoulade sauce.

Preparation & Cooking Tips: Use fresh lump crab meat.

Salmon Patties

Preparation Time: 5 minutes

Cooking Time: 10 minutes

Servings: 4

Ingredients:

- 1 yellow onion, minced
- 15 oz. salmon flakes
- 1 teaspoon dill weed
- ½ cup breadcrumbs
- 1 egg, beaten

Method:

1. Combine onion, salmon, dill weed, breadcrumbs and egg in a bowl.
2. Mix well.
3. Form 4 patties from the mixture.
4. Add the patties to the air crisper tray.
5. Choose air fry setting.
6. Cook at 370 degrees F for 5 minutes per side.

Serving Suggestions: Serve with green salad.

Preparation & Cooking Tips: Refrigerate salmon patties for 1 to 2 hours before air frying to make them firmer and easier to handle.

Chapter 8: Vegetable Recipes

Parmesan Zucchini

Preparation Time: 10 minutes
Cooking Time: 30 minutes
Servings: 4

Ingredients:

- 1 tablespoon olive oil
- 1 tablespoon butter, melted
- 1 teaspoon lemon juice
- 1 teaspoon dried basil
- 1 teaspoon dried parsley
- ¼ cup Parmesan cheese, grated
- 1 teaspoon Italian seasoning
- 1 teaspoon lemon zest
- 2 zucchinis, sliced into rounds

Method:

1. Combine all the ingredients in a bowl.
2. Toss the zucchini to coat evenly with the sauce and herbs.
3. Place the zucchini mixture on top of a foil sheet.
4. Fold and seal.
5. Place the foil packet on the air crisper tray.
6. Set it to air fry.
7. Air fry at 350 degrees F for 30 minutes.

Serving Suggestions: Garnish with lemon slices.

Preparation & Cooking Tips: You can also add a little salt and pepper to the mixture if you like.

Roasted Broccoli Rabe

Preparation Time: 10 minutes
Cooking Time: 8 minutes
Servings: 4

Ingredients:

- 4 cups broccoli rabe
- 2 tablespoons olive oil
- 1 tablespoon lemon juice
- 1 teaspoon garlic powder
- 1 tablespoon Parmesan cheese, grated
- 1/2 teaspoon red pepper flakes
- Salt and pepper to taste

Method:

1. Toss the broccoli in oil and lemon juice.
2. In a bowl, mix the remaining ingredients.
3. Sprinkle mixture all over the broccoli rabe.
4. Add the broccoli rabe to the air fryer oven.
5. Choose air fry function.
6. Cook at 350 degrees F for 5 to 8 minutes.

Serving Suggestions: Sprinkle with crispy garlic bits on top.

Preparation & Cooking Tips: You can also use this recipe for cauliflower or broccoli.

Roasted Garlic

Preparation Time: 5 minutes
Cooking Time: 15 minutes
Servings: 4

Ingredients:

- 1 cup garlic cloves, peeled
- 3 tablespoons olive oil
- Salt and pepper to taste

Method:

1. Drizzle garlic with oil.
2. Season with salt and pepper.
3. Wrap with foil.
4. Place in the air crisper tray.
5. Choose air fry setting.
6. Cook at 370 degrees F for 15 minutes.

Serving Suggestions: Let cool before serving or storing in an airtight container.

Preparation & Cooking Tips: You can also puree roasted garlic and use it in your recipes.

Eggplant Cutlets

Preparation Time: 10 minutes
Cooking Time: 7 minutes
Servings: 4-6

Ingredients:

- 1 eggplant, sliced
- Salt to taste
- 1 egg, beaten
- ¼ cup milk
- 1 cup breadcrumbs

Method:

1. Sprinkle eggplant with salt.
2. Let it sit for 10 minutes.
3. Flip and sprinkle the other side with salt.
4. Add breadcrumbs to a bowl.
5. Beat in the eggs and milk in another bowl.
6. Dip the eggplant in egg mixture.
7. Dredge with breadcrumbs.
8. Add to the air crisper tray.
9. Select air fry setting.
10. Cook at 320 degrees F for 5 minutes.
11. Flip and cook for another 2 minutes.

Serving Suggestions: Serve with marinara dip.

Preparation & Cooking Tips: Use Italian breadcrumbs.

Garlic Roasted Carrots

Preparation Time: 10 minutes
Cooking Time: 12 minutes
Servings: 4

Ingredients:

- 1 lb. carrots, diced
- 2 tablespoons olive oil
- Salt and pepper to taste
- 2 teaspoons garlic powder

Method:

1. Toss the carrots in olive oil.
2. Season with salt, pepper and garlic powder.
3. Coat evenly with the seasoning.
4. Place the carrots in the air crisper tray.
5. Set it to air fry.
6. Cook at 390 degrees F for 12 minutes, stirring once or twice.

Serving Suggestions: Sprinkle chopped parsley on top.

Preparation & Cooking Tips: You can also use baby carrots for this recipe.

Tomato Salad

Preparation Time: 10 minutes
Cooking Time: 3 minutes
Servings: 4

Ingredients:

- 2 cups tomatoes, diced
- ¼ cup red onions, sliced
- 1 tablespoon olive oil, divided
- ½ tablespoon vinegar
- Salt and pepper to taste

Method:

1. Toss the tomatoes in half of olive oil.
2. Add to the air crisper tray.
3. Set your air fryer oven to air fry function.
4. Cook at 350 degrees F for 3 minutes, stirring once.
5. Transfer tomatoes to a bowl.
6. Stir in the rest of the ingredients.

Serving Suggestions: Serve as side dish to a grilled main course.

Preparation & Cooking Tips: Use white wine vinegar for this recipe.

Roasted Asparagus

Preparation Time: 10 minutes
Cooking Time: 10 minutes
Servings: 4

Ingredients:

- 1 lb. asparagus, trimmed and sliced
- 2 tablespoons olive oil
- Salt and pepper to taste
- 2 cloves garlic, minced
- ¼ cup Parmesan cheese, shaved

Method:

1. Toss the asparagus in oil, salt and pepper.
2. Stir in the garlic.
3. Transfer the asparagus to your air crisper tray.
4. Turn the knob to air fry function.
5. Set it to 400 degrees F.
6. Cook for 7 to 10 minutes, stirring once or twice.
7. Sprinkle with the Parmesan cheese.

Serving Suggestions: Sprinkle with a little pepper before serving.

Preparation & Cooking Tips: You can also use garlic power in place of minced garlic.

Roasted Butternut Squash

Preparation Time: 10 minutes
Cooking Time: 10 minutes
Servings: 4

Ingredients:

- 1 butternut squash, sliced into cubes
- 2 tablespoons olive oil
- 2 tablespoons butter, melted
- 2 tablespoons sage, chopped
- Salt and pepper to taste

Method:

1. Toss the butternut squash cubes in olive oil and butter.
2. Season with salt, pepper and sage.
3. Coat evenly with the sauce.
4. Add the squash cubes in the air crisper tray.
5. Cook at 370 degrees F for 10 minutes, stirring.

Serving Suggestions: Serve as side dish to grilled meat main course.

Preparation & Cooking Tips: Use either dried or fresh sage.

Bok Choy Stir Fry

Preparation Time: 5 minutes
Cooking Time: 10 minutes
Servings: 4

Ingredients:

- 2 tablespoons peanut oil
- 2 teaspoons garlic, minced
- 3 tablespoons chicken broth
- 1 tablespoon oyster sauce
- Salt to taste
- 1 lb. bok choy

Method:

1. Mix the peanut oil, garlic, chicken broth, oyster sauce and salt.
2. Stir in the bok choy and coat with the sauce.
3. Add to the air crisper tray.
4. Choose grill function.
5. Cook for 10 minutes, stirring once or twice.

Serving Suggestions: Sprinkle crispy garlic bits on top.

Preparation & Cooking Tips: Use low-sodium chicken broth.

Garlic Mushrooms

Preparation Time: 5 minutes

Cooking Time: 10 minutes

Servings: 4

Ingredients:

- 8 oz. button mushrooms, sliced
- 2 tablespoons olive oil
- 1 teaspoon soy sauce
- 1 teaspoon garlic powder
- Salt and pepper to taste

Method:

1. Toss the mushrooms in olive oil and soy sauce.
2. Sprinkle with the garlic powder, salt and pepper.
3. Arrange the mushrooms in the air crisper tray.
4. Choose air fry setting.
5. Cook at 350 degrees F for 10 minutes, stirring once.

Serving Suggestions: Sprinkle with chopped parsley.

Preparation & Cooking Tips: You can also use minced fresh garlic instead of garlic powder.

Chapter 9: Appetizer Recipes

Ham & Cheese Rolls

Preparation Time: 10 minutes

Cooking Time: 7 minutes

Servings: 8

Ingredients:

- 1 package crescent rolls
- ¼ lb. deli ham
- 1/3 cup cheddar cheese, shredded
- Olive oil

Method:

1. Roll out the crescent dough.
2. Top with the ham and cheese.
3. Roll up the dough.
4. Brush with oil.
5. Place in the air crisper tray.
6. Set the air fryer oven to bake.
7. Bake at 350 degrees F for 7 minutes.

Serving Suggestions: Sprinkle with chopped green onions.

Preparation & Cooking Tips: You can also brush the rolls with butter instead of olive oil.

Salt & Pepper Calamari

Preparation Time: 10 minutes
Cooking Time: 10 minutes
Servings: 4

Ingredients:

- ¼ cup flour
- Salt and pepper to taste
- 1 lb. squid, sliced into rings
- 1 egg, beaten
- Cooking spray

Method:

1. Combine flour, salt and pepper in a bowl.
2. Dip the squid in egg.
3. Dredge with flour mixture.
4. Transfer the squid rings to the air crisper tray.
5. Spray with oil.
6. Choose air fry setting.
7. Cook at 350 degrees F for 5 minutes.
8. Flip and cook for another 5 minutes.

Serving Suggestions: Serve with sweet chili sauce.

Preparation & Cooking Tips: You can also dredge squid breadcrumbs.

Italian Stuffed Mushrooms

Preparation Time: 10 minutes
Cooking Time: 5 minutes
Servings: 10

Ingredients:

- ¼ cup olive oil
- 2 cloves garlic, minced
- ½ cup Parmesan cheese, grated
- ½ cup breadcrumbs
- 2 tablespoons parsley, minced
- Salt and pepper to taste
- 25 mushrooms, stems removed

Method:

1. In a bowl, mix all the ingredients except mushrooms.
2. Stuff the mushroom caps with the mixture.
3. Arrange on a single layer in the air crisper tray.
4. Set the air fryer oven to roast.
5. Cook at 340 degrees F for 5 minutes.

Serving Suggestions: Sprinkle with chopped parsley.

Preparation & Cooking Tips: Use Italian breadcrumbs.

Crab Rangoons

Preparation Time: 5 minutes
Cooking Time: 7 minutes
Servings: 15

Ingredients:

- 8 oz. crab meat
- 8 oz. cream cheese
- 30 egg roll wrappers
- ¼ cup olive oil

Method:

1. Mix crab meat and cream cheese.
2. Top the wrappers with the mixture.
3. Fold up the wrappers and seal.
4. Brush both sides with olive oil.
5. Place the rolls in the air crisper tray.
6. Set it to air fry function.
7. Cook at 300 degrees F for 7 minutes.

Serving Suggestions: Serve with chili garlic sauce.

Preparation & Cooking Tips: Extend cooking time if you want your crab rangoons crispier.

Carrot Chips

Preparation Time: 10 minutes
Cooking Time: 12 minutes
Servings: 6

Ingredients:

- 3 carrots, sliced thinly into rounds
- 2 tablespoons olive oil
- Salt to taste

Method:

1. Coat the carrots with oil.
2. Season with salt.
3. Place the carrots in the air crisper tray.
4. Cook at 360 degrees F for 6 minutes.
5. Flip and cook for another 6 minutes.

Serving Suggestions: Let cool before serving or store in an airtight container.

Preparation & Cooking Tips: You can also season carrots with garlic powder if you like.

Chapter 10: Dessert Recipes

Coffee Mug Cake

Preparation Time: 15 minutes
Cooking Time: 15 minutes
Servings: 1

Ingredients:

- Cooking spray

Cake

- 3 tablespoons all-purpose flour
- 1 tablespoon sugar
- ½ teaspoon baking powder
- ½ teaspoon salt
- 2 tablespoons vegetable oil
- 1 egg, beaten
- ½ teaspoon vanilla extract

Streusel

- 3 teaspoon brown sugar
- 1 teaspoon ground cinnamon
- 1 ½ teaspoons vegetable oil

Method:

1. Coat your coffee mug with oil.
2. Combine the cake ingredients in a bowl.
3. In another bowl, blend the streusel ingredients.
4. Layer the cake and streusel ingredients in your mug.
5. Place the mug inside your air fryer oven.
6. Set it to bake.
7. Bake at 350 degrees F for 12 to 15 minutes.

Serving Suggestions: Let cool for 5 minutes before serving.

Chocolate Cupcake

Preparation Time: 10 minutes
Cooking Time: 15 minutes
Servings: 6

Ingredients:

- 2 cups all-purpose flour
- ¼ cup cocoa powder
- 2 teaspoons baking soda
- 1 cup granulated sugar
- 1 teaspoon vanilla extract
- 1 cup water
- Oil for greasing

Method:

1. Combine all the ingredients in a bowl.
2. Grease your muffin pan with oil.
3. Pour the mixture into the muffin cups.
4. Place in the air fryer oven.
5. Choose bake option.
6. Bake at 320 degrees F for 12 to 15 minutes.

Serving Suggestions: Drizzle with chocolate syrup before serving.

Preparation & Cooking Tips: You can add frosting on top if you like.

Butter Cake

Preparation Time: 10 minutes

Cooking Time: 10 minutes

Servings: 4

Ingredients:

- 14 oz. cookie butter
- 3 eggs
- ¼ cup sugar
- Oil for greasing

Method:

1. Add the cookie butter to a microwave safe bowl.
2. Microwave for 90 seconds, pausing every 30 seconds to stir.
3. Mix the melted cookie butter with the eggs and sugar.
4. Beat until fully combined.
5. Grease your ramekin with oil.
6. Pour the mixture into the ramekin.
7. Set the ramekin in the air fryer oven.
8. Choose air fry function.
9. Cook at 320 degrees F for 10 minutes.

Serving Suggestions: Let cool before slicing and serving.

Preparation & Cooking Tips: Top with heavy cream and chopped walnuts if you like.

Cinnamon Apple Chips

Preparation Time: 5 minutes

Cooking Time: 10 minutes

Servings: 4

Ingredients:

- 3 apples, sliced thinly
- ¼ cup butter, melted
- 1 tablespoon ground cinnamon

Method:

1. Coat the apple slices with the butter.
2. Sprinkle with ground cinnamon.
3. Add the apple slices to the air fryer oven.
4. Cook at 300 degrees F for 15 minutes, flipping once.

Serving Suggestions: Let cool before serving.

Preparation & Cooking Tips: Use a mandolin to slice the apples thinly.

Grilled Watermelon

Preparation Time: 5 minutes
Cooking Time: 6 minutes
Servings: 4

Ingredients:

- 2 tablespoons lime juice
- 1 tablespoon olive oil
- Pinch salt
- 1 watermelon, sliced

Method:

1. Mix lime juice, oil and salt in a bowl.
2. Brush watermelon slices with this mixture.
3. Place watermelon slices in the air crisper tray.
4. Choose grill setting.
5. Cook at 400 degrees F for 2 to 3 minutes per side.

Serving Suggestions: Garnish with mint leaves.

Preparation & Cooking Tips: Use ripe watermelon for this recipe.

Chapter 11: 30-Day Meal Plan

Day 1

Breakfast: Cinnamon French toast

Lunch: Chicken with veggies

Dinner: Roast beef

Day 2

Breakfast: German pancake

Lunch: Cajun tilapia

Dinner: Grilled steak

Day 3

Breakfast: Scrambled egg toast

Lunch: Szechuan chicken

Dinner: Pork roast

Day 4

Breakfast: Breakfast quesadillas

Lunch: Korean fried chicken

Dinner: Roasted leg of lamb

Day 5

Breakfast: Quiche Lorraine

Lunch: Roasted chicken

Dinner: Korean Beef

Day 6

Breakfast: Breakfast tuna melt

Lunch: Bok choy stir fry

Dinner: Blackened pork chops

Day 7

Breakfast: Ricotta toast

Lunch: Parmesan zucchini

Dinner: Roast beef

Day 8

Breakfast: Egg toast with cheese

Lunch: Bacon pudding with corn

Dinner: Herbed tilapia

Day 9

Breakfast: Baked apple toast

Lunch: Rib eye steak

Dinner: Spicy fried chicken

Day 10

Breakfast: German pancake

Lunch: Spicy ribs

Dinner: Grilled steak

Day 11

Breakfast: Cheesy biscuits

Lunch: Flank steak

Dinner: Roasted salmon

Day 12

Breakfast: Scrambled egg toast

Lunch: Beef teriyaki

Dinner: Herbed lamb

Day 13

Breakfast: Breakfast quesadillas

Lunch: Lemon crab cake

Dinner: Vietnamese pork rolls

Day 14

Breakfast: Egg toast with cheese

Lunch: Crispy cod fillet

Dinner: Lamb with garlic and rosemary

Day 15

Breakfast: Cinnamon French toast

Lunch: Blue cheese burger

Dinner: Cajun chicken

Day 16

Breakfast: Quiche Lorraine

Lunch: Indian butter shrimp

Dinner: Pork Teriyaki

Day 17

Breakfast: Breakfast tuna melt

Lunch: Giant burger

Dinner: Paprika chicken

Day 18

Breakfast: Ricotta toast

Lunch: Tomato salad

Dinner: Steak with garlic and butter

Day 19

Breakfast: Egg toast with cheese

Lunch: Salmon patties

Dinner: Grilled steak

Day 20

Breakfast: German pancake

Lunch: Lime chicken

Dinner: Spicy ribs

Day 21

Breakfast: Scrambled egg toast

Lunch: Honey lemon salmon

Dinner: Pork and mushrooms

Day 22

Breakfast: Baked apple toast

Lunch: Greek lamb chops

Dinner: Savory pork loin

Day 23

Breakfast: Cheesy biscuits

Lunch: Korean Beef

Dinner: Vietnamese pork rolls

Day 24

Breakfast: Breakfast quesadillas

Lunch: Roasted salmon

Dinner: Indian butter shrimp

Day 25

Breakfast: Cinnamon French toast

Lunch: Steak roulade

Dinner: Stuffed chicken

Day 26

Breakfast: Quiche Lorraine

Lunch: Giant burger

Dinner: Lamb with garlic and rosemary

Day 27

Breakfast: Baked apple toast

Lunch: Stuffed shrimp

Dinner: Rib eye steak

Day 28

Breakfast: Breakfast tuna melt

Lunch: Crispy cod fillet

Dinner: Herbed lamb

Day 29

Breakfast: Cheesy biscuits

Lunch: Breaded pork chop

Dinner: Sesame chicken

Day 30

Breakfast: Ricotta toast

Lunch: Honey lemon salmon

Dinner: Grilled lamb chops

Conclusion

Air fryers are already awesome gadgets.

But its big brother, the air fryer oven, might be better. With its many functionalities, the Power Air Fryer 360 can potentially replace most of your kitchen appliances. It has many presets, a sleek design, and includes free cooking accessories.

But where the Power Air Fryer 360 shines is its roasting capabilities. The unit comes with a rotisserie spit. The interior's extra-large capacity lets you roast up to four pounds of meat that is beautifully brown on the outside and tender on the inside.

From simply making stale chips crispy again to roasting delicious pork for dinner, the Power Air Fryer 360 surely gets the job done.